Sylke Burger

# DAS WUT-MUT-BUCH

Ein interaktives Mitmachbuch für Groß und Klein

## WUTI-ZONG wird mutig!

VERLAG
BASIC ERFOLGSMANAGEMENT

Impressum

Das WUT-MUT-Buch
WUTI-ZONG wird mutig
© 2019 basic erfolgsmanagement
www.basic-erfolgsmanagement.de
Alle Rechte vorbehalten

ISBN: 978-3-944987-22-4

Text: Sylke Burger, Kindheitspädagogin (B.A.)
Illustration und Gestaltung:
Michaela Adler, Dipl.-Designerin (FH)
Lektorat: Lena Kempfler,
Medienbüro Susanne Wagner, Pfarrkichen
Übersetzungsbüro: Ü-Werk GmbH, Landshut

Made in Germany

Ein  von:

.................................................................................................

Von  für:

.................................................................................................

Dieses Buch ist entstanden mit
freundlicher Unterstützung von educcare

„educcare hat mir als Kindheitspädagogin zwischen 2015 und 2017
die entscheidende Tür geöffnet, sinnvoll und nachhaltig mit Kindern
und Eltern in Deutschland zu arbeiten. Gleichzeitig hat educcare
mir eine fünf-monatige Auszeit gewährt, in der ich mich ehrenamtlich
in Südafrika engagiert habe. Beides war grundlegend für dieses Buch,
das auch in Zusammenarbeit mit den Kindern der educcare-Kita in
Hennef entstanden ist." Sylke Burger

www.educcare.de

Vielen Dank an alle Spenden-und Ideengeber!

Andrea Bauer, Regina Beck, Ulla Bielefeld, Mathias Burger, Renate und Rainer Burger, Derick Edube, Nadine Farella, Katrin Feldmann, Mona Griesbeck, Kristina Horn, Inge Koch, Michelle Menke, Beatrice und Estelle Müller, Diana Ottinger, Eva Posywio, David Ramirez, Anja Reisdorf, Kati Rode, Sabina Stern, Axel Thelen, Sally Webersinke, den Kindern, Mamas und Papas auf dieser Welt, dem Team des Parent Centres in Südafrika und allen, die an der Verbreitung des Buches mithelfen!

# WUTI-ZONG

Weiß was er will und was er nicht will, schreit aber laut, ist oft verletzend oder schlägt zu – das sind seine Feuerbälle.

Kopf ist heiß –

Schreit laut

Herz schlägt schnell

Wirft Feuerbälle

Trommelt mit den Fäusten

Bauch tut weh

Stampft wild mit den Füßen

## WUT-GEFÜHLSREISE

- Was ist Wut?
- Was macht Dich wütend?
- Was machst Du, wenn Du wütend bist?
- Wie fühlt sich Dein Körper an, wenn Du wütend bist? (Kopf, Stimme, Hals, Herz, Bauch, …)

Begeben Sie sich mit dem Kind auf die Wut-Mut-Gefühlsreise. Gerne können Sie die MUT-Brille zusammen mit Ihrem Kind selbst gestalten und spielerisch in die Geschichte einbauen! Die Vorlagen finden sie auf S. 32.

# MUTI-ZONG

Auch MUTI-ZONG weiß, was er will und was er nicht will!
Er traut sich das mutig zu sagen. Bleibt aber klar und in Ruhe.

Mut-Brille
zum Selbermachen
auf Seite 32.

Hat eine Mut-Brille:
damit macht er Dinge,
die er sich eigentlich
nicht traut.

Denkt nach, bevor
er spricht

Atmet tief ein
und aus

Er verschenkt
Mut-Bälle

Sagt mutig,
was er will

Steht ruhig und
sicher auf dem
Boden

## MUT-GEFÜHLSREISE

• Was ist Mut?
• Wann warst Du mutig?
• Wann hast Du das letzte Mal
  etwas Mutiges gemacht?
• Wie fühlt sich Dein Körper an,
  wenn Du mutig bist?
  (Kopf, Stimme, Hals, Herz,
  Bauch, ...)

7

Die kleine Marie sitzt
mit ihrer Mama
am Frühstückstisch.
Marie nimmt ihr Wasserglas
und spielt damit.
Mehrmals sagt Mama:
„Marie, bitte lass' das sein!"
Marie stoppt kurz und spielt
weiter mit dem Glas …

Kannst Du Dir vorstellen was
jetzt passiert?

8

KLIRRRRRRRRRR!!!!
Das Wasserglas
zerbricht in viele
Scherben.

Während Mama immer
wieder sagte: „Marie, bitte
lass' das sein!" bemerkte sie nicht,
dass WUTI-ZONG auf ihre Schulter
kletterte und immer wütender
wurde! Jetzt fängt er an, mit
den Beinen zu stamp-
fen und hält heiße
Feuerbälle in
seinen Fäusten.

Wenn WUTI-ZONG bei Mama ist, kann sie ihre Wut nicht mehr kontrollieren. WUTI-ZONGs Herz rast jetzt ganz schnell, sein Kopf ist heiß und er wirft nun Feuerbälle auf Marie.

Marie hat große Angst und ist traurig.

10

Kennst Du das Wutmonster?
WUTI-ZONG kennt
keine Grenzen! Er wirft
Feuerbälle auf der
ganzen Welt.

Marie sitzt traurig in ihrem Zimmer. „Warum kommt WUTI-ZONG so oft zu Mama? Was kann ich bloß tun?"

Plötzlich entdeckt Marie eine bunte Brille neben sich auf dem Tisch. Sie funkelt in den schönsten Regenbogenfarben. Wo kommt die denn her?

12

Sofort setzt Marie die funkelnde
Brille auf die Nase.
Ooooh! Und was passiert
jetzt?

13

Plötzlich steht Marie auf einer grünen Wiese in einem bunten Land.
Das ist das MUTI-Land!

Alle Kinder, Mamas und Papas tragen diese funkelnde Brille.
Sie singen und spielen. Sie sagen und tun Dinge, die sie sich
sonst nicht trauen. Die Brille ist eine MUT-Brille.

Keine Spur von WUTI-ZONG! Oder wer ist das dort?
Aus dem WUTI-ZONG Monster ist ein starker
MUTI-ZONG geworden. Er lächelt Marie an.

Marie fragt die Kinder: „Kennt ihr auch
den wütenden WUTI-ZONG?"

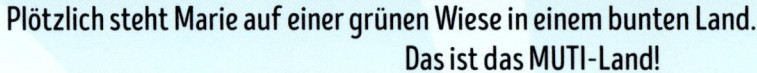

MUTI-LAND

15

Aber klar doch -
WUTI-ZONG wütet doch
auf der ganzen Welt!

NORDAMERIKA

EUROPA

CARMEN
kennt den WUTI-ZONG von zu
Hause aus Amerika. Dort warf er,
zusammen mit ihrem großen
Bruder, heiße Feuerbälle auf sie.

AKON
kennt WUTI-ZONG aus
seiner Heimat Afrika.
Hier hat der WUTI-ZONG
seines Vaters Feuerbälle
auf ihn geworfen.

SÜDAMERIKA

ASIEN

AFRIKA

AUSTRALIEN

**MINZU** kennt den wütenden WUTI-ZONG aus ihrer Heimat China. Die Feuerbälle kamen aus Mamas Mund und taten sehr weh.

**PAUL**
erlebte WUTI-ZONG zu Hause in Australien. Hier haben sich die bösen Worte seiner Freunde in Feuerbälle verwandelt. Das hat ihn sehr traurig gemacht.

17

Die MUT-Brille hat den Kindern geholfen
den wütenden WUTI-ZONG in den mutigen
MUTI-ZONG zu verwandeln. Mit MUTI-ZONG an ihrer
Seite trauen sie sich, Dinge zu tun und zu sagen, die
sie sich vorher nicht getraut haben.

**AKON** aus Afrika ist jetzt stark
und mutig. Laut und deutlich sagt
er zum Vater: „STOPP! LASS'
DAS SEIN!"

**CARMEN**
aus Amerika sagt nun
mutig zu ihrem Bruder:
„Hör' auf zu schlagen!
Sag' mir einfach was los ist!"

18

**PAUL** aus Australien hat für seine Freunde mutige Worte gefunden: „Hört auf, böse Dinge über mich zu sagen! Das tut mir weh."

**MINZU** aus China atmet tief ein und aus: „Sag' mir bitte ruhig, was du von mir möchtest!" Damit kann sie die Feuerbälle stoppen.

Marie ist glücklich. Sie hat eine Idee! Was kann das sein?

# WUTI-LAND

Marie nimmt ihre MUT-Brille ab und steht direkt bei Mama und WUTI-ZONG im dunklen WUTI-Land. Mama ist immer noch traurig und sagt zu Marie: „Es tut mir so leid. Ich hatte Streit mit Papa und so viel Arbeit. Da habe ich nicht gemerkt, dass WUTI-ZONG auf meine Schulter geklettert ist."

20

Mut-Brille
zum Selbermachen
auf Seite 30.

Muti-Zong
wird mutig!

„Ach Mama!", sagt Marie. „Mit meiner neuen MUT-Brille komme ich gerade aus dem MUTI-Land! Dort habe ich MUTI-ZONG und viele mutige Kinder, Mamas und Papas getroffen." Mama sagt: „Marie, können wir gemeinsam eine MUT-Brille für mich und meinen WUTI-ZONG basteln?" „Au ja, Mama! Dann kommst auch du ins schöne MUTI-Land und alles wird gut!"

21

Gesagt, getan! Mit großen Augen und mit der MUT-Brille steht Mama plötzlich im MUTI-Land. Sie hört sich die Geschichten der starken Kinder und mutigen Mamas und Papas an.

**AKONS PAPA**
erzählt seine Wut-Mut-Geschichte.
Er hat mutig anderen Mamas und
Papas von seinem WUTI-ZONG erzählt.
Sie haben ihm geholfen. seinen
WUTI-ZONG in MUTI-ZONG zu verwandeln.

**CARMENS BRUDER**
hat auf seine Schwester gehört.
Die heißen Feuerbälle seines
WUTI-ZONGS haben sich in gute
Worte verwandelt.

23

## PAULS FREUNDE

haben verstanden, dass sie ihm wehgetan haben. Das wollen sie nicht mehr und spielen jetzt fröhlich mit ihm.

**1,2,3...**

## MINZUS MAMA

erzählt, dass sie dreimal tief ein- und ausatmet und die Wut fühlt. Ihr Atmen und Fühlen löscht das Feuer und verwandelt WUTI-ZONG in MUTI-ZONG.

24

Mama hat eine Idee. Wenn WUTI-ZONG auf ihre Schulter klettern will, dann wird sie eine MUT-Ampel spielen:

**STOPP**

Rot bedeutet, WUTI-ZONG zu stoppen und erstmal bis zehn zu zählen!

**FÜHLEN**

Gelb heißt, dreimal tief ein- und ausatmen und die Wut im Körper zu fühlen.

**MUT**

Grün steht für den Mut, ruhig zu sagen, was ich will oder nicht will.

Gemeinsam singen nun alle den WUT-MUT-Song. Er bringt sie zusammen mit der MUT-Brille jederzeit ins MUTI-Land zurück.

# DER WUT-MUT SONG

WUTI-ZONG, ZONG, ZONG! Feuert Ping Pong, Pong, Pong!
Ich fühle Wut, Wut, Wut! Heiß wie die Glut, Glut, Glut!
Mein Kopf ist heiß, heiß, heiß! Es läuft der Schweiß, Schweiß, Schweiß!
Mein Herz das rennt, rennt, rennt! Mein Bauch der brennt, brennt, brennt!
Die Wut ist da, da, da! Ich nehm' Dich wahr, wahr, wahr!

*(Wer mag, kann jetzt die selbstgebastelte Mut-Brille aufsetzen!)*

Stopp, lass' das sein! Mich anzuschrei'n!
Geh' erstmal raus! Aus meinem Haus!
Ich atme ein - ich atme aus!
Und wieder ein - und wieder aus!
Die Wut ist raus, raus, raus! Applaus, Applaus, plaus, plaus!
Die Wut ist raus, raus, raus! Applaus, Applaus, plaus, plaus!

MUTI-ZONG - ZONG - ZONG! Macht fröhlich Klong, Klong, Klong!
Ich fühle Mut, Mut, Mut! Und das tut gut, gut, gut!
Mein Kopf ist frei, frei, frei! Die Wut vorbei, bei, bei!
Mein Herz ganz leicht, leicht, leicht! Mein Bauch ganz weich, weich, weich!
Der Mut ist da, da, da! Hurra, Hurra, ra, ra!
Der Mut ist da, da, da! Hurra, Hurra, ra, ra!

Den Wut-Mut-Song
und viele weitere Infos
findest Du unter:
www.wutmut.com

27

Wie sieht Dein WUTI-ZONG aus?
Male ihn hier auf!

Wie sieht Dein MUTI-ZONG aus?
Male ihn hier auf!

## SO BLEIBEN WIR IN KONTAKT!

Vielen Dank für den Kauf des WUT-MUT-Buches und dass Sie sich mutig mit Ihrem Kind auf die Gefühlsreise begeben haben. Über Ihr Feedback und Ihre Ideen freue ich mich unter: sylke.burger@wutmut.com

Weiterführende Information für Eltern, Erzieher und Kita-Leitung erhalten Sie auf meiner Projektseite:

# www.wutmut.com

• Download MUT-Brillen
• Download Malseiten
• Download WUT-MUT Song
• Elternchat und Elternratgeber
• Projektangebote für Kitas

Webseiten, die weiterhelfen:
• www.robert-betz.com
• www.selbstbehauptung-vorschulkinder.de
• www.theparentcentre.org.za

*Herzlichst, Ihre Sylke Burger*

# ÜBER DIE AUTORIN

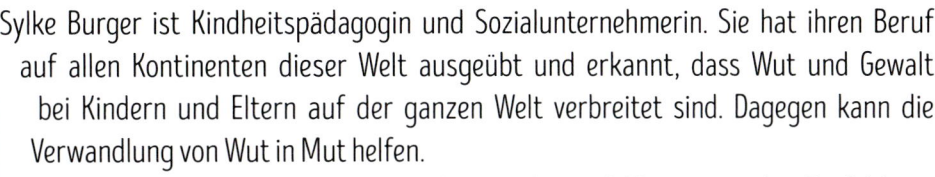

Sylke Burger ist Kindheitspädagogin und Sozialunternehmerin. Sie hat ihren Beruf auf allen Kontinenten dieser Welt ausgeübt und erkannt, dass Wut und Gewalt bei Kindern und Eltern auf der ganzen Welt verbreitet sind. Dagegen kann die Verwandlung von Wut in Mut helfen.

Mit diesem Buch stärkt sie nachhaltig Kinder und Eltern, um den Teufelskreis aus Wut und Gewalt zu durchbrechen. Sie erkennt Wut als eine wichtige und wertvolle Kraft an. Es ist ihr ein Herzenswunsch, mit diesem Buch ihre pädagogische Erfahrung in Form von einfachen Praxistipps an Kinder und Eltern weiterzugeben.

Sylke Burger engagiert sich seit vielen Jahren für die Bildung von Eltern und Kindern auf der ganzen Welt, organisiert Charity-Events und spendet einen Teil ihres Einkommens für The Parent Centre in Südafrika. Auch von diesem Buch fließen 15% des Erlöses an die Organisation, welche sich nachhaltig für die Stärkung von Eltern gegen Gewalt an Kindern einsetzt (www.theparentcentre.org.za).

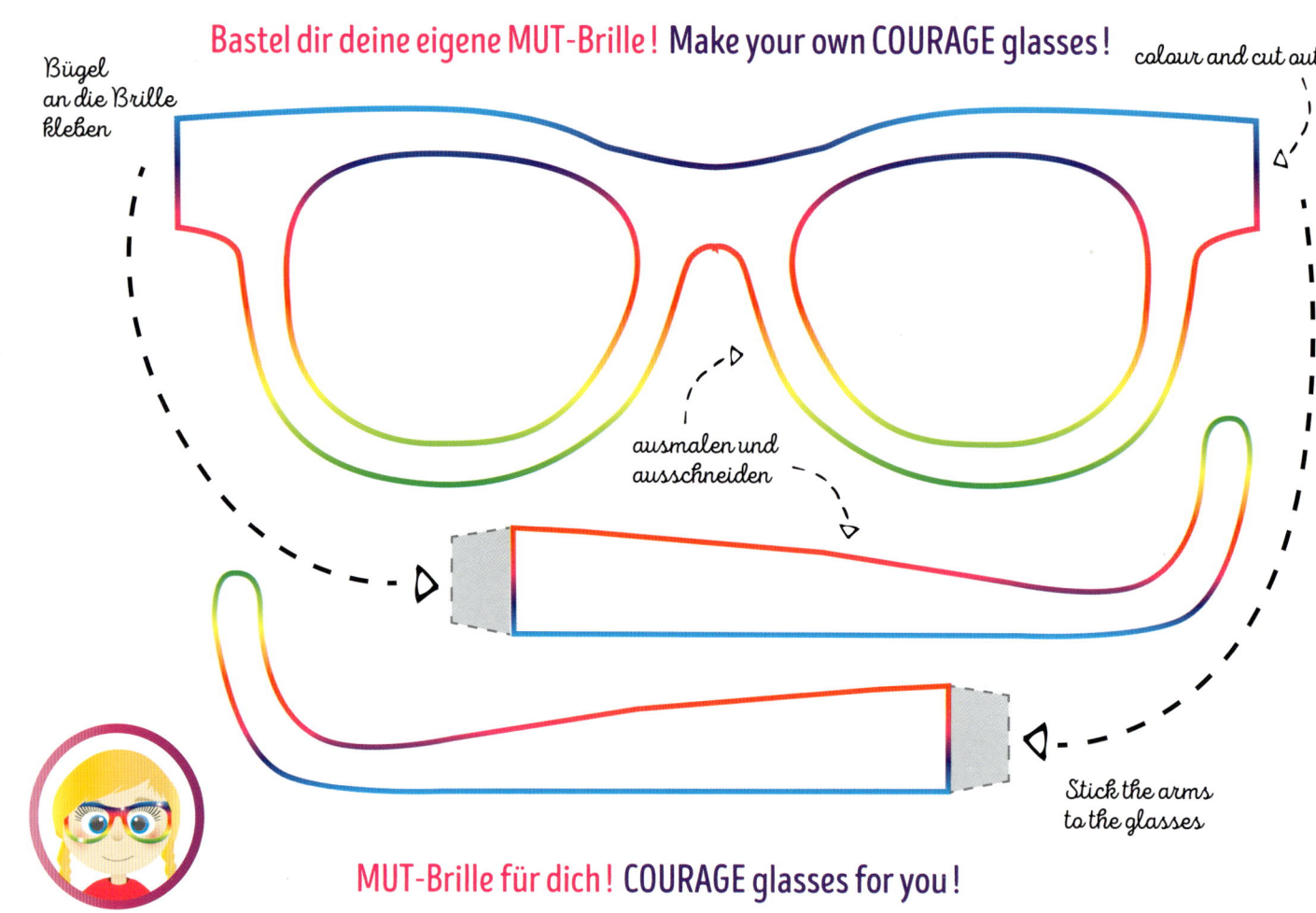

Bastel dir deine eigene MUT-Brille! Make your own COURAGE glasses!

colour and cut out

Bügel an die Brille kleben

ausmalen und ausschneiden

Stick the arms to the glasses

MUT-Brille für dich! COURAGE glasses for you!

# THE ANGER-COURAGE BOOK

Sylke Burger

## An interactive book for all ages

**WUTI-ZONG becomes courageous!**

PUBLISHER
BASIC ERFOLGSMANAGEMENT

Imprint

The ANGER-COURAGE Book
WUTI-ZONG becomes courageous!
© 2019 basic erfolgsmanagement
www.basic-erfolgsmanagement.de

ISBN: 978-3-944987-22-4

Text: Sylke Burger,
Kindheitspädagogin (B.A.) - Early Childhood Educator
Illustration and design:
Michaela Adler, Graduate Designer (FH)
Proofreading: Lena Kempfler
Medienbüro Susanne Wagner, Pfarrkichen
Translation: Ü-Werk GmbH, Landshut

Made in Germany

A  from:

.......................................................................................

From  for:

.......................................................................................

This book was written with
friendly support from educcare

"As an Early Childhood Educator between 2015 and 2017, educcare
opened up crucial doors to meaningfully and long-term work
with children and parents in Germany. At the same time, educcare
gave me a 5-month sabbatical during which I volunteered in South
Africa. Both were fundamental for this book, which was also written
in cooperation with children from the educcare childcare centre
in Hennef." Sylke Burger

www.educcare.de

Thank you to everyone who donated and contributed their ideas!

Andrea Bauer, Regina Beck, Ulla Bielefeld, Mathias Burger, Renate and Rainer Burger, Derick Edube, Nadine Farella, Katrin Feldmann, Mona Griesbeck, Kristina Horn, Inge Koch, Michelle Menke, Beatrice and Estelle Müller, Diana Ottinger, Eva Posywio, David Ramirez, Anja Reisdorf, Kati Rode, Sabina Stern, Axel Thelen, Sally Webersinke, the children, the mums and dads of this world, the team at The Parent Centre in South Africa and everyone who is helping to get the book out there!

# WUTI-ZONG

knows what he wants and what he doesn't want, but he shouts, is often hurtful or hits out - these are his fireballs.

Hot head

Shouts

Heart beats fast

Throws fireballs

Bangs his fists

Tummy aches

Stomps his feet wildly

6

## ANGER'S EMOTIONAL JOURNEY

- What is anger?
- What makes you angry?
- What do you do when you're angry?
- How does your body feel when you're angry? (head, voice, throat, heart, tummy, …)

Set off on the anger-courage emotional journey with your child. You are welcome to make the COURAGE glasses together with your child and integrate them into the story in a playful way! You can find the templates on page 30.

# MUTI-ZONG

MUTI-ZONG also knows what he wants and what he doesn't want! He has the courage to say this out loud. But clearly and calmly.

Make your own courage glasses on page 32.

Thinks before he speaks

Takes a deep breath in and out

Has courage glasses: with these he does things that he doesn't actually have the courage for.

He gives away courage balls

Bravely says what he wants

## COURAGE'S EMOTIONAL JOURNEY

- What is courage?
- When were you courageous?
- When was the last time you did something courageous?
- How does your body feel when you're courageous?
  (head, voice, throat, heart, tummy, ...)

Stands quietly and firmly on the floor

7

Little Marie is sitting
with her mum at the
breakfast table.
Marie takes her water
glass and plays with it.
Mum says several times,
"Marie, please don't do that!"
Marie stops briefly and then
continues playing with the glass ...

Can you imagine what
happens next?

SMASHHHH!!!! The water glass shatters into lots of pieces.

While Mum kept saying, "Marie, please don't do that," she didn't notice that WUTI-ZONG was climbing onto her shoulder and getting angrier and angrier! Now he's starting to stomp his feet and is holding hot fireballs in his fists.

9

When WUTI-ZONG is with Mum, she can't control her anger any more. WUTI-ZONG's heart is racing really fast now, his head is hot and he's throwing fireballs at Marie.

Marie is very scared and sad.

10

Do you know the anger monster?
WUTI-ZONG has no boundaries!
He throws fireballs all
over the world.

Marie is sitting sadly in her room. "Why does WUTI-ZONG come to Mum so often? What can I do?"

Suddenly Marie discovers a pair of colourful glasses next to her on the table. They sparkle with the most beautiful rainbow colours. Where did they come from?

12

Marie puts on the sparkling
glasses straight away.
Oooooh! And what
happens now?

13

Suddenly Marie is standing in a green meadow in a colourful country.
This is COURAGE land!

All the children, mums and dads are wearing these sparkling glasses.
They are singing and playing. They are saying and doing things
they would not have the courage to do otherwise.
These are COURAGE glasses.

There's no trace of WUTI-ZONG! Or who's that there?
The WUTI-ZONG monster has turned into a strong
MUTI-ZONG. He smiles at Marie.

Marie asks the children,"do you also
know the angry WUTI-ZONG?"

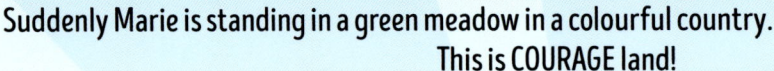

14

COURAGE LAND

But of course -
WUTI-ZONG rages
all over the world!

NORTH AMERICA

EUROPE

**CARMEN**
knows the WUTI-ZONG from her
home in America. Together with
her big brother, he threw hot
fireballs at her.

**AKON**
knows WUTI-ZONG
from his home in Africa.
WUTI-ZONG threw
his father's fireballs
at him here.

SOUTH AMERICA

16

ASIA

AFRICA

AUSTRALIA

**MINZU** knows the angry WUTI-ZONG from her home in China. The fireballs came out of her mum's mouth and hurt a lot.

**PAUL**
met WUTI-ZONG at home in Australia. This is where his friends' nasty words turned into fireballs. That made him very sad.

17

The COURAGE glasses helped the children to turn the angry WUTI-ZONG into the courageous MUTI-ZONG. With MUTI-ZONG by their side, they are brave enough to do and say things they didn't dare to before.

**AKON** from Africa is now strong and brave. He says loudly and clearly to his father, "STOP! LEAVE ME ALONE!"

**CARMEN** from America now bravely says to her brother, "Stop hitting me! Just tell me what's wrong!"

18

**PAUL** from Australia found courageous words for his friends, "Stop saying nasty things about me! They are hurtful."

**MINZU** from China takes a deep breath in and out, "Please just calmly tell me what you want from me!" This stops the fireballs.

Marie is happy.
She has an idea!
What could it be?

19

# ANGER LAND

Marie takes off her COURAGE glasses and is instantly standing with her mum and WUTI-ZONG in dark ANGER land. Mum is still sad and says to Marie, "I'm so sorry. I had a fight with Dad and so much work. I didn't realise that WUTI-ZONG had climbed onto my shoulder."

20

Make your own
courage glasses
on page 32.

Muti-Zong
becomes
courageous!

"Oh, Mum!" says Marie, "with my new COURAGE glasses I've just come from COURAGE land! I met MUTI-ZONG and many courageous children, mums and dads there." Mum says, "Marie, can we make some COURAGE glasses for me and my WUTI-ZONG?" "Oh, yes, Mum! Then you can come to beautiful COURAGE land too and everything will be fine!"

21

No sooner said than done! With wide eyes and COURAGE glasses, Mum suddenly finds herself in COURAGE land. She listens to the strong children and brave mums and dads telling their stories.

**AKON'S DAD**
tells his anger-courage story.
He bravely told other mums
and dads about his WUTI-ZONG.
They helped him turn his
WUTI-ZONG into a MUTI-ZONG.

**CARMEN'S BROTHER**
listened to his sister.
His WUTI-ZONG'S hot fireballs
have turned into kind words.

23

## PAUL'S FRIENDS

have understood that they hurt his feelings. They don't want to do that any more and are now playing happily with him.

1,2,3...

## MINZU'S MUM

tells us that she takes a deep breath in and out three times and feels her anger.
Her breathing and feeling put out the raging fire and turn WUTI-ZONG into MUTI-ZONG.

24

Mum has an idea! When WUTI-ZONG wants to climb on her shoulder, she'll play a courage traffic light game:

**STOP**

Red means stopping WUTI-ZONG by counting to ten first!

**FEEL**

Amber means taking a deep breath in and out three times and feeling the anger in her body.

**COU-RAGE**

Green stands for the courage to calmly say what she wants or doesn't want.

Everyone now sings the ANGER-COURAGE song together. The song and the COURAGE glasses take them back to COURAGE land at any time.

26

# THE ANGER-COURAGE SONG

WUTI-ZONG, ZONG, ZONG! Fires Ping Pong, Pong, Pong!
Feeling so mad, mad, mad! Makes others sad, sad, sad!
My head is hot, hot, hot! Heats up a lot, lot, lot!
My heart beats boom, boom, boom! Belly goes zoom, zoom, zoom!
Anger is here, here, here! And also fear, fear, fear!

*(If you want to, put on your homemade courage glasses now!)*

Stop, let it be! Screaming at me!
Why can't you see! It's hurting me!
I am breathing in and  breathing out!
And breathing in and breathing out!
Anger is out, out, out! Shout it loud, loud, loud!
Anger is out, out, out! Shout it loud, loud, loud!

You can find the
Anger-Courage song
and more information at:
www.angercourage.com

MUTI-ZONG, ZONG, ZONG! So very strong, strong, strong!
I feel so brave, brave, brave! See how I  wave, wave, wave!
My head is free, free, free! Cool like iced tea, tea, tea!
My heart is light, light, light! Belly feels right, right, right!
Courage each day, day, day! Hooray, hooray, ray, ray!
Courage each day, day, day! Hooray, hooray, ray,  ray!

What does your WUTI-ZONG look like?
Draw it here!

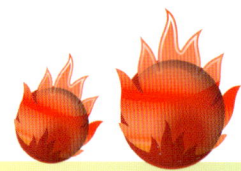

 **What does your MUTI-ZONG look like?**
**Draw it here!**

29

# HOW TO STAY IN TOUCH!

Thank you very much for purchasing the ANGER-COURAGE book and courageously embarking on an emotional journey with your child. I would be thrilled to receive your feedback and ideas at: sylke.burger@angercourage.com

You can find more information for parents, educators and daycare managers on my project page:

## www.angercourage.com

- Download the COURAGE glasses
- Download the drawing pages
- Download the ANGER-COURAGE song
- Parent chat and parent guide
- Project offers for childcare centres

Helpful websites:
- www.robert-betz.com
- www.selbstbehauptung-vorschulkinder.de
- www.theparentcentre.org.za

*Kind regards, Sylke Burger*

## ABOUT THE AUTHOR

Sylke Burger is an Early Childhood Educator and social entrepreneur. She has worked on all the world's continents and recognised that anger and violence are common among children and parents all over the world. Transforming anger into courage. With this book she is empowering children and parents to permanently break the vicious circle of anger and violence. She sees anger as an important and valuable force. It is her firm hope that with this book she can pass her experience in education onto children and parents in the form of simple practical tips.

Sylke Burger has been involved in educating parents and children around the world for many years, organising charity events and donating part of her income to "The Parent Centre" in South Africa. 15% of the proceeds from this book will also be donated to this organisation, which is committed to sustainably empowering parents to combat violence towards children (www.theparentcentre.org.za).

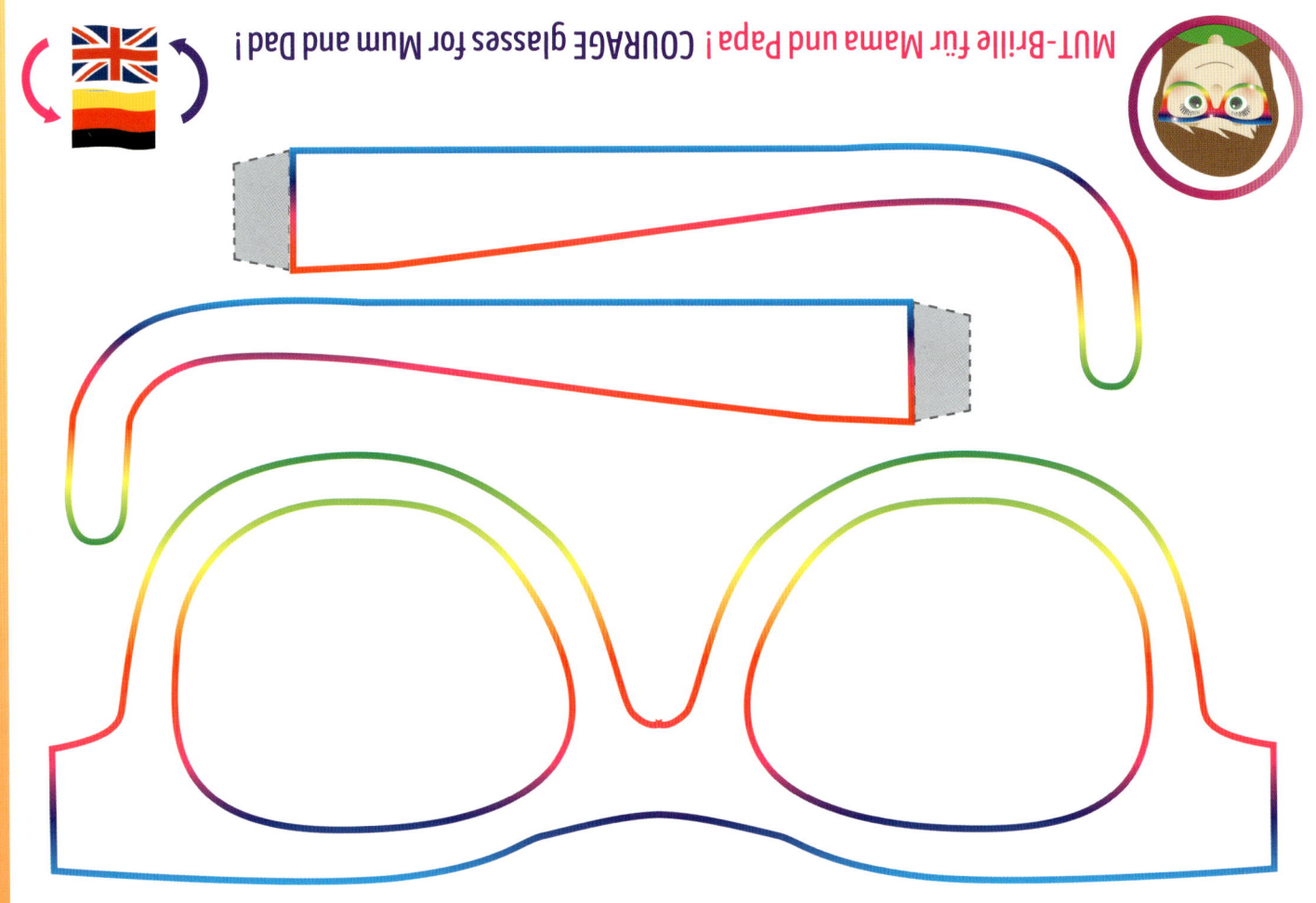